Scissor Skills

Cut & Paste

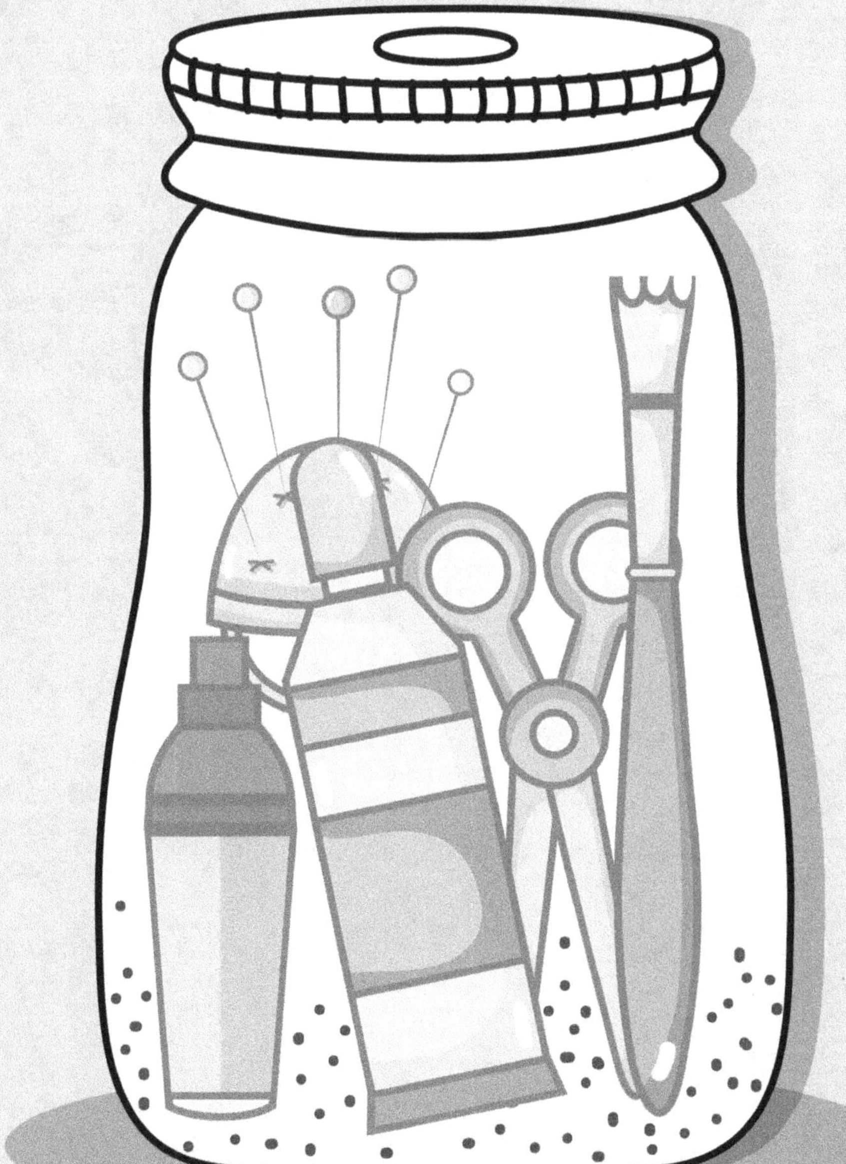

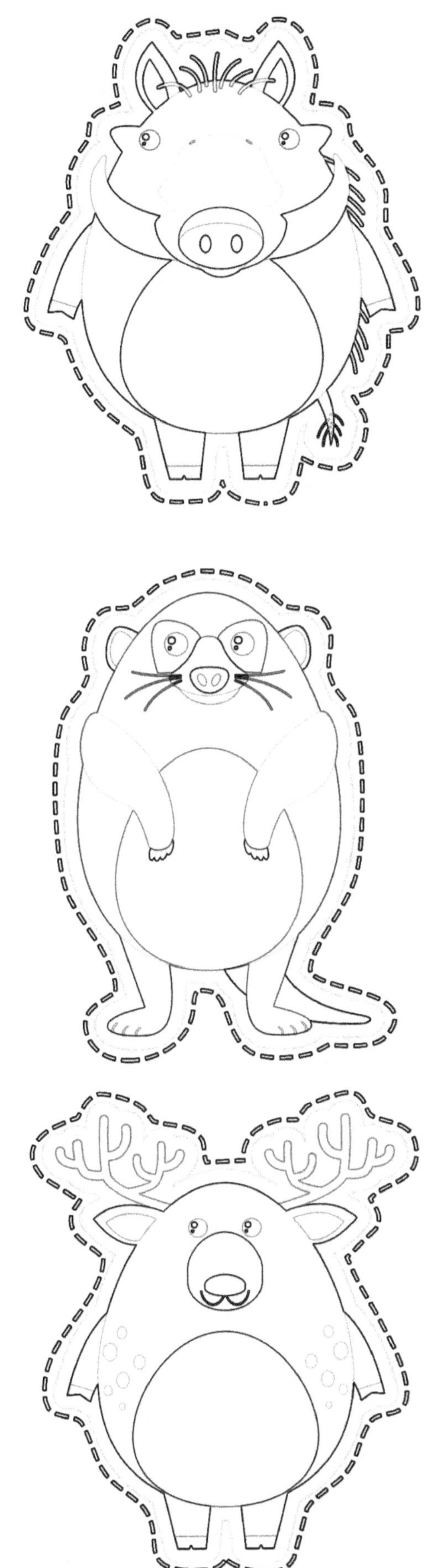

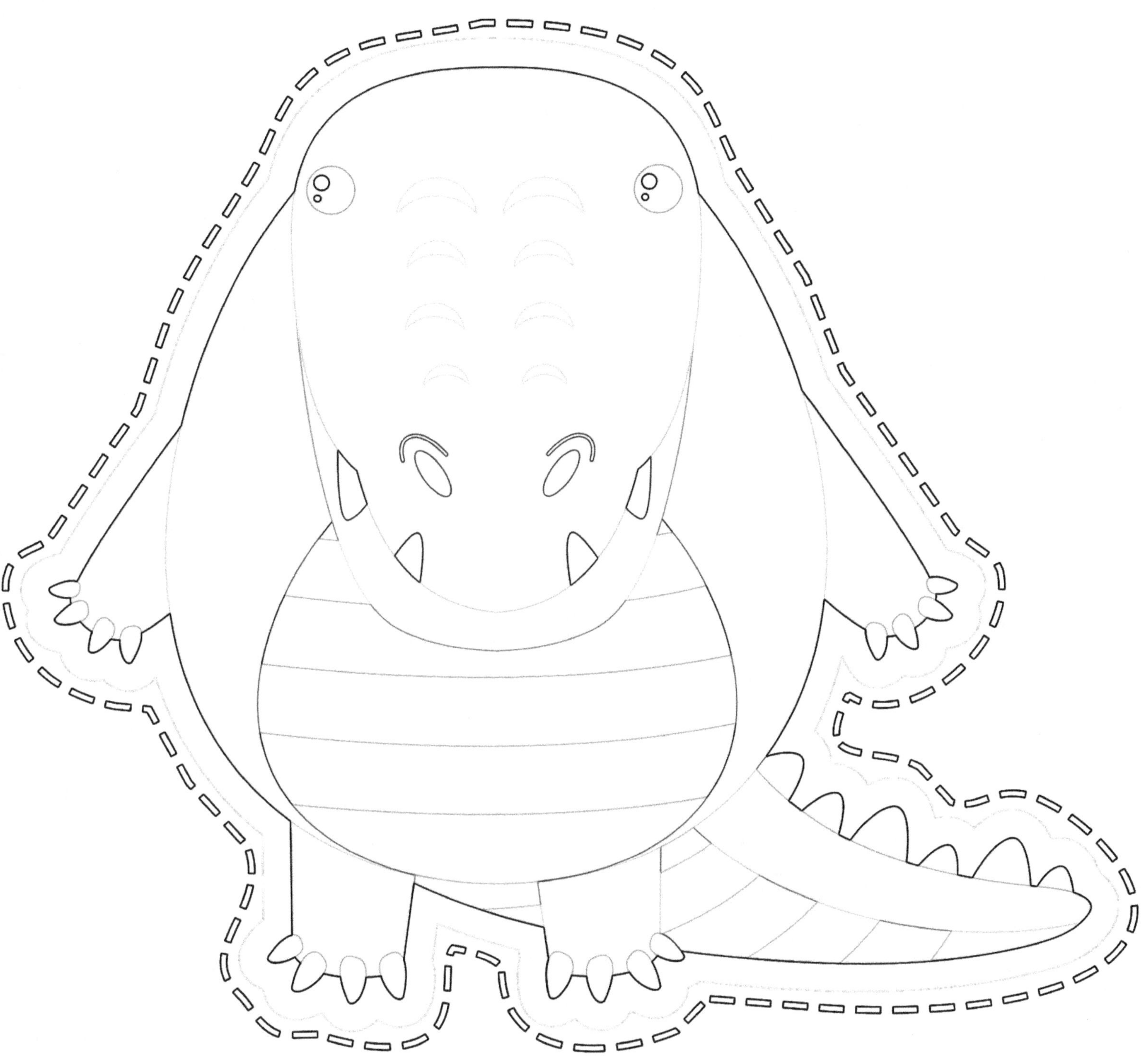

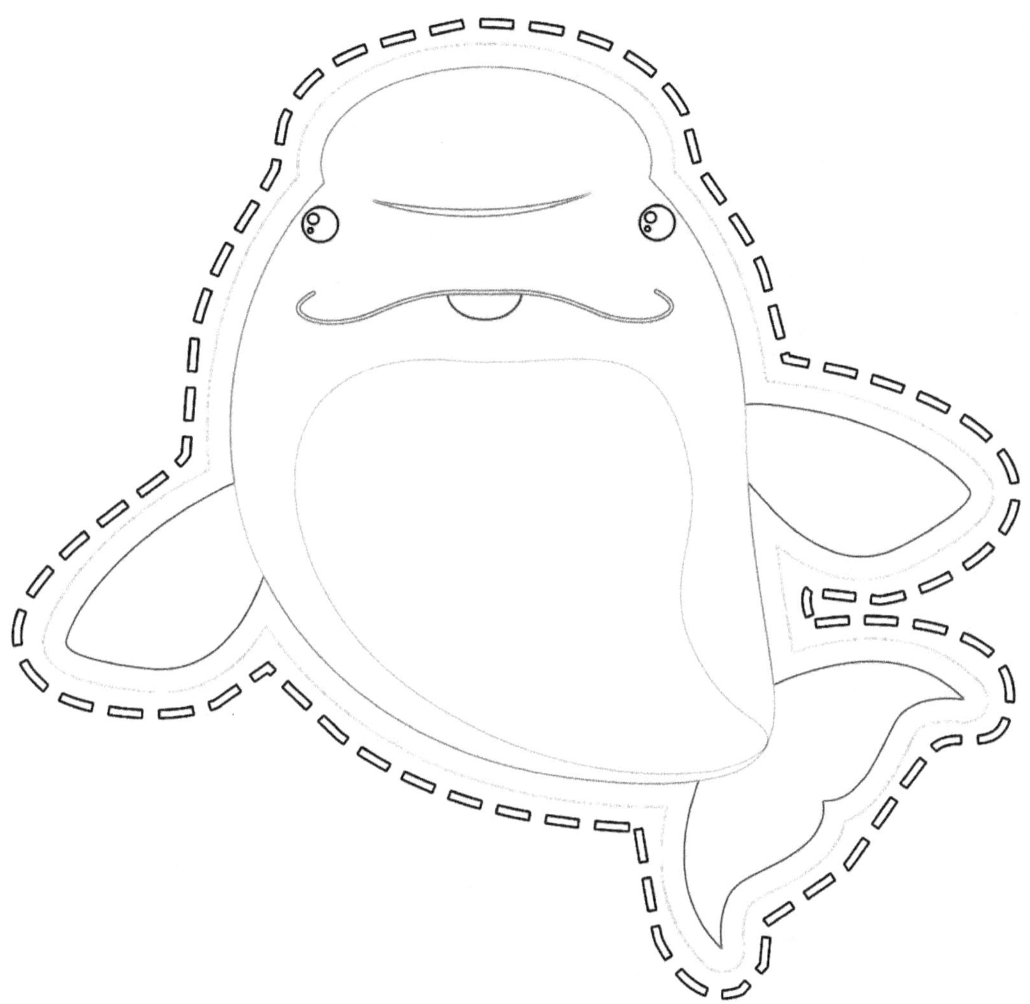

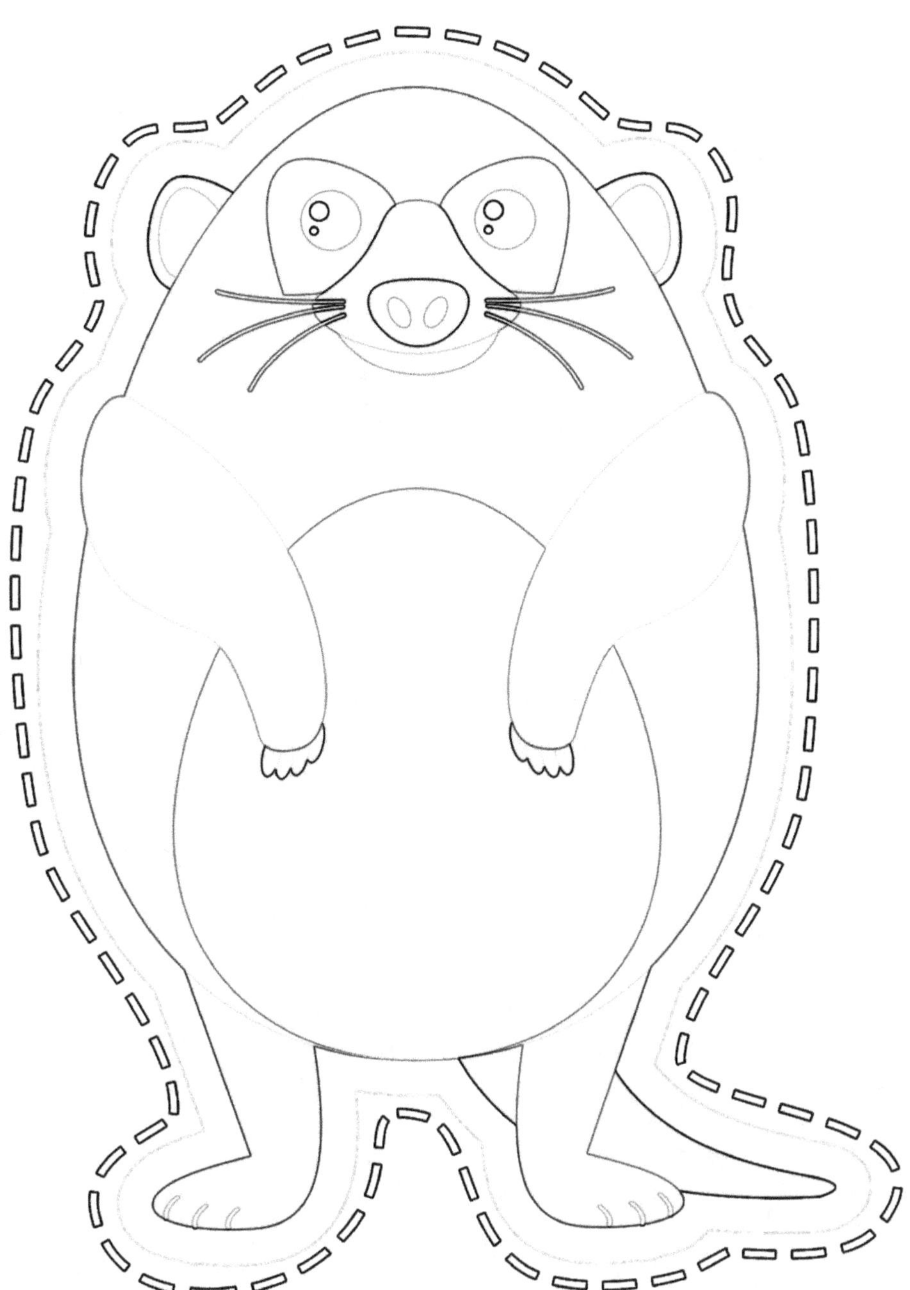

FARM

FARM

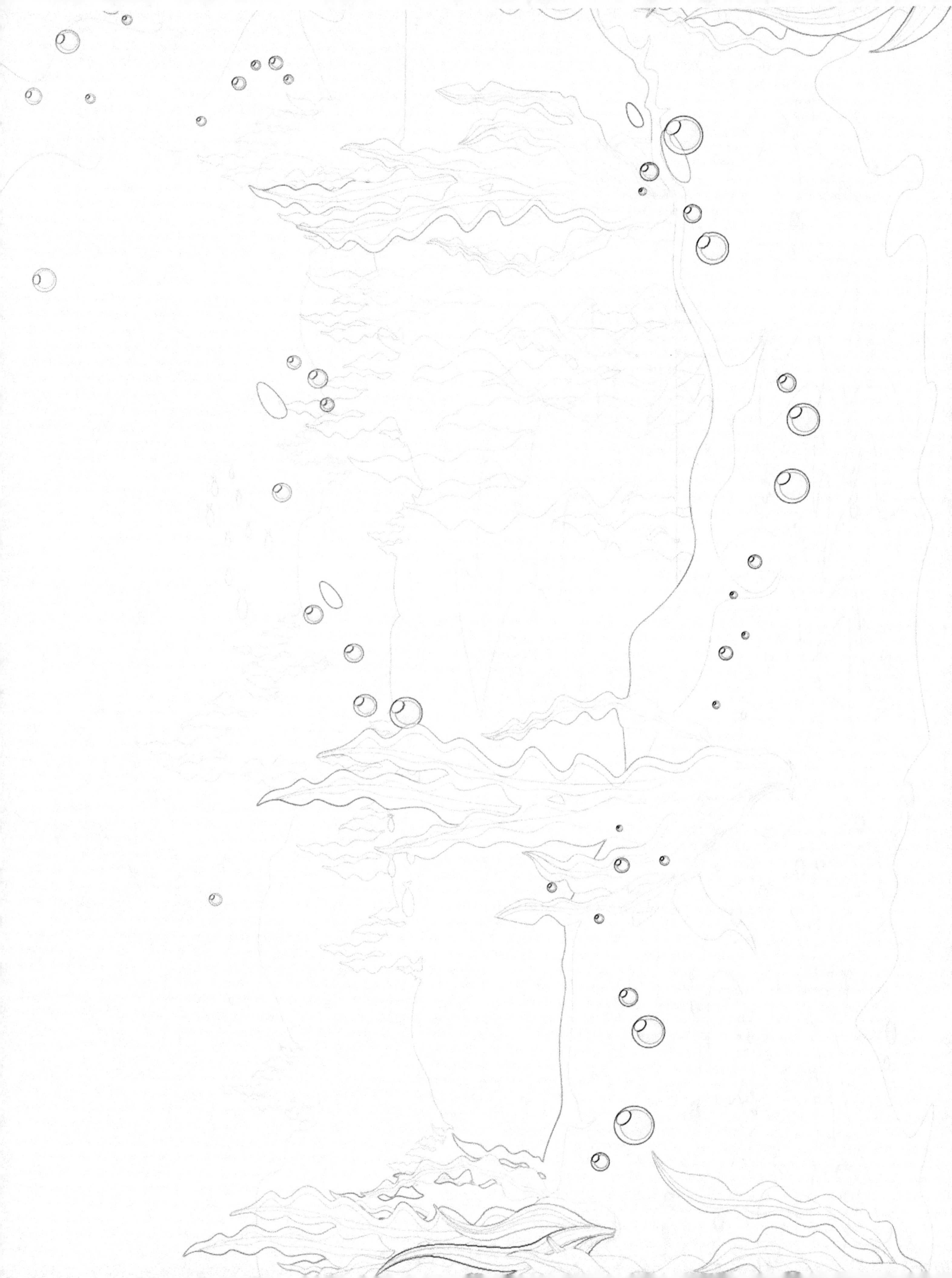